Little Author
in the
BIG WOODS

N
W
E
S
Places Laura Lived
SOUTH DAKOTA
De Smet
MINNESOTA
Walnut Grove
WISCONSIN
Pepin
Burr Oak
IOWA
NEBRASKA
MISSISSIPPI RIVER
MISSOURI
KANSAS
Independence
Mansfield
(Rocky Ridge)
Area of Detail
Scale of Miles
0
100
200

Little Author
～ in the ～
BIG WOODS

A Biography of
Laura Ingalls Wilder

Yona Zeldis McDonough
illustrations by Jennifer Thermes

Christy Ottaviano Books
Henry Holt and Company
New York

Henry Holt and Company, LLC
Publishers since 1866
175 Fifth Avenue
New York, New York 10010
mackids.com

Henry Holt books may be purchased for business or promotional use. For information on
bulk purchases, please contact Macmillan Corporate and Premium Sales Department at
(800) 221-7945 x5442 or by e-mail at specialmarkets@macmillan.com.

Library of Congress Cataloging-in-Publication Data
McDonough, Yona Zeldis.
Little author in the big woods : a biography of Laura Ingalls Wilder / Yona Zeldis
McDonough ; illustrated by Jennifer Thermes. — First edition.
pages   cm
Summary: "Many girls in elementary and middle school fall in love with the Little House
books by Laura Ingalls Wilder. What they don't always realize is that Wilder's books are
autobiographical. This narrative biography describes more of the details of the young
Laura's real life as a young pioneer homesteading with her family on many adventurous
journeys. This biography, complete with charming illustrations, points out the differences
between the fictional series as well as the many similarities. It's a fascinating story of a
much-celebrated writer"—Provided by publisher.
Includes bibliographical references.
ISBN 978-0-8050-9542-5 (hardback) — ISBN 978-1-62779-279-0 (e-book)
1. Wilder, Laura Ingalls, 1867–1957—Juvenile literature. 2. Women authors, American—
20th century—Juvenile literature. 3. Women pioneers—United States—Biography—
Juvenile literature. 4. Wilder, Laura Ingalls, 1867–1957. Little house books—Juvenile
literature. 5. Autobiographical fiction, American—History and criticism—Juvenile
literature. I. Thermes, Jennifer, illustrator. II. Title. III. Title: Biography of
Laura Ingalls Wilder.
PS3545.I342Z7684 2014   813'.52—dc23 [B]   2014014946

First Edition—2014/Designed by Ashley Halsey
Printed in the United States of America by R. R. Donnelley & Sons Company,
Harrisonburg, Virginia

1 3 5 7 9 10 8 6 4 2

For Katherine Constance McDonough,
darling daughter, beautiful girl

—Y. Z. M.

For Kirsten

—J. T.

~ CONTENTS ~

Little Author
in the
BIG WOODS

Author's Note

Many writers have used people, places, and events from their own lives to form their fiction. But Laura Ingalls Wilder was a writer who used the events of her life to form the basis of her novels in a more direct way. She changed hardly anything about her past when she recast it into fiction; she even used her own name and the names of her family members, so that the character Laura Ingalls of the Little House series shares her name with her creator, Laura Ingalls

Wilder. The same is true for her sisters, friends, neighbors, and teachers. She did change the last name of the unkind girl from Owens to Oleson, and she chose not to include the death of her baby brother. But mostly, Wilder used her life as the basis for the wonderful books she wrote. In this biography, readers of the Little House books will recognize many events and details from the fictional versions; it is my hope that knowing the facts that inspired the stories will deepen an understanding of these much-loved classics.

Yona Seldin McDonough

Prologue

In 1839, Caroline Lake Quiner was born in the Milwaukee, Wisconsin, area. Some people said she was the first non–Native American baby to be born there. Her parents, Henry and Charlotte, were pioneers who had come from the east to settle the new land. It was not uncommon for pioneers to move many times. Sometimes they were pulled in a new direction by the promise of fertile or free land, or new job opportunities. Other times they were pushed away from a place by disease, drought, or other calamities.

Even though Caroline's early life was hard (and it became even harder after her father drowned), her mother, Charlotte, believed in the importance of education, even for girls. This was a very unusual idea for the time. Women were expected to tend house and raise children, so girls were taught to cook, clean, sew, and garden. "Book learning" was a luxury that most girls were not given. But Charlotte had been educated at a female seminary in Connecticut, and she wanted her daughters to have book learning too.

Little Caroline was a star pupil. She loved to read, and she excelled at writing essays and poetry. A schoolteacher who boarded with the family praised Caroline's compositions. So when Caroline told her mother she wanted to follow in her footsteps and become a teacher, she not only had Charlotte's support, she had her blessing.

At 16, Caroline finished school and passed the examination for her first teaching certificate. She was hired to teach at the very same school where she and her sisters and brothers had been students. Her salary was somewhere between $2.50 and $3.00 a week. Though the wages were modest, she was proud to be earning money of her own. She used her salary to buy clothes and to help her parents and siblings.

Even out on the frontier, Caroline had a sense of grace and elegance. She may have been a country girl, but she didn't have country manners. Her unusual poise caught the eye of a neighbor's son, Charles Ingalls. They began "keeping company"—an old-fashioned term for dating—and were married in Concord, Wisconsin, on February 1, 1860. She had not yet turned 21 years old.

Caroline understood that her new husband craved adventure. And he understood that, although she would indulge his craving and

follow him willingly on his travels, her refined nature would set the tone for the life they led together. Wherever they went, Caroline was a lady.

In 1863, Charles and Caroline followed some members of the Ingalls family to the Big Woods of Wisconsin, near the village of Pepin. Charles and his brother-in-law Henry Quiner built two rough-hewn log cabins, not too far apart from each other. It was important to have family nearby. They helped each other with the building and with other chores as well. The cabin

Henry shared with his wife, Polly, was busy and noisy—they had three children. In contrast, the cabin shared by Charles and Caroline was a much calmer and quieter place.

All that changed in 1865. Just as the Civil War between the North and the South was ending, Caroline gave birth to a baby girl she named Mary. Two years later, Laura came along. Now Caroline had two little girls and a bustling, noisy cabin of her own. But no matter where she went and what hardships she endured, she never lost that special sense of grace, and she imbued her daughters with her own rare spirit.

As much as Laura loved her strong, cheerful blue-eyed father, who could play the fiddle and fix just about anything, she was deeply shaped by the women around her—her mother and her sisters, Mary, Caroline (born in 1870), and Grace (born in 1877). It was these strong, resourceful pioneer women who became her role models. And in the end, it was these same women who helped define and populate the fictional world of the Little House books, for which she became so well known and loved. Laura learned so much from her mother—lessons that lasted a lifetime. But even more important were the tender feelings she had for her mother, which she described this way: "dearer than Mother's teachings are little personal memories: Mother's face, Mother's touch, Mother's voice."

ONE

Early Journeys

1870–1871
Wisconsin–Kansas–Wisconsin

The Wisconsin woods were very big. The house was very small. Laura Elizabeth Ingalls was small too, a little girl in the big, big woods. She lived in a log cabin with her Pa, Ma, and older sister, Mary Amelia. The trees surrounding the house stood proud and tall. Oak, ash, and elm. Maple, butternut, and birch. The dense woods were home to many of the animals Pa hunted and trapped for their meat and skins. He farmed, too, in the clearings where the forest opened up and the land was exposed to the sun and the wind.

To Laura, the woods around the cabin must have seemed vast and endless. There were no other houses, buildings, or streets, just the trees and the occasional sight of an owl as it flapped its great wings against the sky. In the winter, glittering white snow piled up against the sides of the cabin. In spring, the woods and fields were filled with flowers.

Laura and Mary played outside, watched by their Ma and Jack, the fiercely loyal spotted bulldog that was their family pet. They had no reason to think of leaving. Everything they ever needed or wanted was right there.

But Pa had other ideas. He had a yen

to go out west. He wanted even more land, more space, and more opportunity. He'd heard that out west there were deer, antelope, prairie chickens, and wild turkeys. The land was level and the soil fertile. And best of all, it was free! In 1862,

Congress had passed the Homestead Act. This meant that the United States government was offering 160 free acres of land to people willing to settle on the prairie and farm for at least five years.

Once Pa learned that, he was all set to pack up and leave Pepin behind. But in the Ingalls family, Pa and Ma made all the big decisions together. In the evenings, after the chores were done, they sat by the table and talked over the pros and cons. They would be leaving their families behind. The trip was dangerous. Ma loved their snug little cabin and saw no reason to leave it. Pa pointed out that the land cost nothing. They could farm and make money. He could afford to build a frame house, and to buy a buggy and a team of horses. He promised Caroline fine clothes and jewelry too. Long into the night they talked. And the next night, and the night after that. Soon it was decided. They would go to Kansas!

Once they made the decision, preparations for the long trip began. First Pa had to fit a white, waterproof canvas over their wagon's curved bows. The wagon would become their home while on their journey, and even after they arrived; it would take some time to build a new house and they would need shelter in the meantime.

Then Ma started on the packing. Into the wagon went their clothes, dishes, books, and bedding. Patchwork quilts and tablecloths, pots and pans. Pa's fiddle rode up front, cushioned on a pile of quilts. In late April 1870, everything was ready. Ma, Pa, Mary, and Laura said good-bye to all their rela-tives. Then they climbed into the wagon, with faith-ful Jack following alongside. Pa drove the horses to the

edge of Lake Pepin. Fortunately, the lake was still covered in ice, so they could get the wagon across it. On the other side of the lake was Minnesota.

For weeks they lived in the wagon, crossing the state of Minnesota, then traveling south through Iowa and Missouri, and finally heading west into the wide-open state of Kansas. Laura was too little to remember the trip. But Ma and Pa told her so many stories about it that the stories became a part of her. Eventually, it was as if she *did* remember the covered wagon, the unfamiliar landscape filled with woods, hills, creeks, and rivers, and the little rabbits that hid in the grass and prairie chickens that fluttered in the road.

It was a long and hard journey. Sometimes it poured. Other times it was blisteringly hot. But when they stopped for the night, Pa played his fiddle and Ma cooked a good supper over the

campfire. Even on the lonely, desolate prairie, Ma managed to make the girls feel at home.

The family came to the Verdigris River, and when the horse pulled the wagon across, they found themselves in the frontier town of Independence, Kansas. But Pa had not come all this way to settle in a town. He wanted the expansive spaces of the prairie. They got back in the wagon and continued on for another 13 miles southwest. He kept looking until he found a spot that seemed just right. It was near a stream. The stream played a big part in his decision because they needed to be near water. And the trees that grew along the banks could be used to build their house and provide wood for a fire.

Pa started in on the new house straight away. First he had to find the right trees—only the straightest ones would do. Next he had to cut them down and haul them to the building site in his wagon. It took several days to prepare enough logs—about 50 logs in all. Then he started to build. Day by day the walls of the new cabin grew higher, and then higher still. When it was high enough, he made a temporary skeleton roof from slender saplings. Over this he tied the canvas wagon cover. Later he would put on a more secure roof, made from wooden logs that had been split into thin slabs. But there were other, more important things to do first. He had to dig a well. And he had to build a log barn, to protect the horses from thieves and from the packs of wolves that roamed the prairie.

After the building came the backbreaking work of plowing. Although Pa often traded work with neighbors for help with building, he worked long days alone in the fields with his sod plow, breaking up the tough grasslands into fields where he could plant. He planned to grow wheat, potatoes, corn, and other crops. The tall grass was thick and not easy to cut. The underground root system was so strong that Pa had to get off the plow and hack it with his ax. But he was strong and determined. He got the job done.

Laura and Mary were too little to help with building a house or plowing the land, and Ma could not do much because she was watching them. But as the girls grew older, they pitched in more and more.

Although Ma and Pa didn't meet too many settlers, they did meet Native Americans, who in those days were called Indians. They did not know it then, but they had settled on an Indian reserve. Sometimes the Indians they saw came to their cabin and asked for food. Other times they just barged right in and took it. Ma never tried to stop them. She and Pa thought it best to try to get along with their Indian neighbors, not fight with them.

One day when Laura was three, Pa took her and Mary on a long walk in the prairie. He was taking them to see an Indian camp. The Indians were all off on a hunting trip, so the camp was empty. But Laura and Mary were excited to find the ashes where the fires had been, and the holes from the tent poles. Then Laura saw something bright shining up from the dust. When she leaned down to pick it up, she saw that it was a bead. And look, there were more of them! Red, green, and blue beads, strewn around the camp. Since the beads were scattered all over, it didn't seem like the Indians cared too much about them, and it didn't feel like stealing. Laura and Mary filled their apron pockets. Pa helped. They didn't leave until the sun started to go down.

Laura couldn't wait to show Ma the beads. She would be so surprised. But Ma had her own surprise. They found her dozing in bed, holding the girls' brand-new baby sister with jet-black hair in her arms! Mrs. Scott, a neighbor, had helped with the delivery. Back then there were few hospitals. Babies were born at home with help from family members, friends, or neighbors.

Ma named the new baby Caroline Celestia and decided they would call her Carrie. Life with the new baby was even busier. Ma had all her regular chores of cooking, cleaning, washing, and mending. Added to that was taking care of the baby.

Soon Ma and Pa noticed that the Indians were showing up more often. They were from the Osage tribe. Pa had not known that he had built the cabin along one of their old trails. He had been in such a hurry to start that he hadn't filed a proper claim on the land. If he had, he might have chosen to build somewhere else.

The Indians were angry with the white settlers for moving onto their land. There was talk that the Indians might decide to wage war on them. Night after night, Laura and her family could hear their loud chanting and war cries. The sound was terrifying—even worse than the howling of wolves.

Meanwhile, far away in Washington D.C., the government was trying to decide what to do about the Indians. Over the years, white settlers had been forcing them off their ancestral lands, and there was now a lot of tension between the two groups. Feeling threatened, the Indians were attacking the settlers. The settlers were retaliating against the Indians. Something had to be done.

In 1870, Congress voted to pay the Osage $1.25 an acre for their land in Kansas. They also voted to give them new land in Oklahoma. The Osage accepted their offer. They would leave Kansas and head to Oklahoma.

Laura and her family were watching on the day the Indians left. To Laura, the long line of Osage on foot and horseback was fascinating. She loved the different-colored ponies and was curious about the children riding bareback. Some of them didn't even wear clothes!

After the Indians left, things settled down. No more surprise visitors. No more war cries in the night. Fall turned to winter, and the Ingalls family all came down with whooping cough. Kindly Dr. Tann—an African-American doctor who had treated the Osage—came to help. A lot of folk cures were prescribed for whooping cough: eating the skin of a snake, drinking white ant tea, tying a bag of live bugs around the throat.

Perhaps Dr. Tann used some of these methods to cure Laura and her family. Perhaps not. Whatever he did, it worked, because they survived and got well again. Soon after they had recovered, Pa got a letter from Gustaf Gustafson, the man who had bought their house in the Big Woods. Mr. Gustafson had been paying off his debt a little at a time, but he was unable to keep up with the payments. Instead, he wanted to head west and asked Pa if he would take the house back.

Ma thought of the time and effort that they had put into their prairie home. What a waste it had been. But Pa didn't see it that way. He thought of the hunting in the Big Woods and the fishing in Lake Pepin. He was willing to go back and reclaim their former home.

As they always did, Ma and Pa talked the

matter over. And in the end, the lure of the journey won out. The covered wagon would be packed up once more, and the Ingalls family would make their way back to Wisconsin.

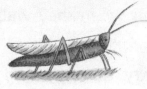

Grasshoppers and a New Baby Brother

1871–1876
Wisconsin–Minnesota–Iowa

The 1871 trip home in the covered wagon took many weeks. Laura was almost five, and this time she remembered more of the journey. When they finally got back to the Big Woods, the Gustafsons were still living in their house, so they moved in with Uncle Henry and Aunt Polly. Laura liked living with her cousins— they had so much fun playing together.

Laura was not quite old enough to join Mary

and her cousins when they walked half a mile down the road to the Barry Corner School. But when Mary returned, she showed Laura everything she had learned. Soon Laura was reading as well as her big sister. Ma and Pa loved reading too. Often, Ma read aloud to Pa in the evenings. She read novels, biographies, and a book about the holy city of Jerusalem called *The Land and the Book.* Laura always associated reading and books with the gentle sound of her mother's voice.

In the fall, Laura was finally old enough to go to school with her sister and cousins. How exciting! She and Mary had a shiny new dinner pail and shared a schoolbook. Their teacher

was named Annie Barry. Although she was only 25 years old, she knew how to keep order in her classroom. Life in the Big Woods was more social than life on

the prairie. Not only did Laura get to play with other children at school, so many friends and relatives stopped by the house to share a meal or to visit. Sometimes there were dances, and Ma would get all dressed up. Laura loved how fine and pretty she looked. When the music started, Pa chimed in with his fiddle. Laura and the other children stood back and watched as the caller shouted out the steps for the dancers to follow.

The Ingalls family felt safe and happy for the next few months. Laura had lots of playmates.

She was especially drawn to Clarence Huleatts, who had red hair and freckles. He liked all the same things she did: running, jumping, and climbing. Mary preferred his little sister, Eva, who had excellent manners. Laura didn't care for Eva so much.

While Laura and Mary were busy with school and friends, Pa farmed and hunted, like he always had. But soon the yearning to head west again took hold of him. He missed the wide-open sky and the plains of Kansas. Once again, Ma wasn't so keen on the idea. She thought their life in the Big Woods was just fine and told Pa he had an "itching toe." But when Pa was able to persuade his brother Uncle Peter and his wife, Aunt Eliza, to join them, Ma changed her mind. She liked the idea of having family along on the journey.

Pa sold his farm in the fall of 1873 to a Swedish man named Anderson for $1,000. The Ingalls family moved in with Aunt Eliza and Uncle Peter until it was time to go. And in February 1874, the two families set off together. Pa wanted to settle in the western part of Minnesota. Since it was too cold to travel across the state in the winter, he and Uncle Peter took over an abandoned cabin in southeastern Minnesota where the two families could stay until spring, when the weather warmed up. Uncle Peter found a farm along the Zumbro River and decided to settle with his family there. But Pa felt the need to keep going, so the Ingalls family continued west without them.

They made their way across the prairie lands until they reached western Minnesota. Finally they came to a village called Walnut Grove. It was no more than a few stores and houses, loosely spread around the railroad tracks. The first railroad linking the East and West coasts of the United States had been completed in 1869. Laura had never been on a train, but she'd been enchanted by the sound of its whistle. While

in town, Pa heard about a Norwegian settler who had travel plans of his own. He was willing to sell his homestead to Pa.

Pa bought the 172 acres of prairie land along Plum Creek. It came with an underground house called a dugout. The small, one-room dugout was carved right into the ground. The roof was made of willow boughs covered by sod, which is grass-covered ground. It was hidden from view except for the stovepipe sticking up through the sod. The walls, made of packed earth, were smoothed and whitewashed. The floor was earth too. Right by the door was a window covered not with glass but with greased paper. It let in only a little bit of light.

Since they were so close to town, Laura and Mary were able to go to school. Although there was no church when the family arrived, Ma joined a committee to help build one. Pa contributed money for the church bell, and when

the church was completed, the Ingalls family attended Sunday services. Laura always remembered the very first decorated Christmas tree in church. The tree held presents for everyone. To Laura, the fur cape and china box she received as gifts were precious.

Minnesota winters were long and hard. Blizzards lasting three or four days whipped across the plains. When this happened, Laura and Mary had to do their lessons at home. But there was a bright side to blizzard season. All the moisture in the ground made for good crops. In the spring of 1875, Pa planted wheat. He was so confident about the crop that he went into town and came back with a load of yellow pine lumber that had been sent to the prairie by railroad. He also came back with glass windows, factory-milled doors, and white china doorknobs. Pa was going to build a house! The shopkeepers all knew about his big wheat field.

He would pay them when he harvested his crop.

One of their neighbors, Eleck Nelson, helped Pa with the framing, the roofing, the windows, and the walls. Laura thought the new house was wonderful. She and Mary had a hard time keeping Pa's secret surprise for Ma: her very own cookstove. Laura and her family were thrilled to move into the new house. All summer long, Pa tended the wheat field. What a crop they would have!

Then, one day, a dark cloud passed in front of the sun. The cloud turned out to be an invasion of grasshoppers. The sky filled with them, and the whirring of their wings made a loud, terrible drone. When they hit the ground, it sounded like a hailstorm. Once they hit, they began to eat: all the wheat Pa had grown, all the vegetables in Ma's garden. Leaves, grass, flowers, and fruit. They stripped the fields and prairie bare. The government tried to fight back: they offered children up to $1.00 for every bushel of dead grasshoppers they collected, and 50 cents for a gallon of their eggs.

Despite the terrible grasshopper devastation to their farm, Pa and Ma were not ready to abandon it. So, before the harvest in late August, Pa walked 200 miles across Minnesota to find work. He was not alone; dozens of men and boys went too, all desperate to make some money.

They were housed and fed by local farmers who took pity on them.

While Pa was gone, Ma and the girls stayed behind, living in a rented house behind the church, where life would be easier when the winter came. It was hard for Ma to be alone. She had to be both mother and father to the girls. She waited anxiously for word from Pa, and when the first letter came, she cried with relief. Pa came home in the fall, his purse filled with money.

On November 1, 1875, Laura's family welcomed a new baby brother, Charles Frederick Ingalls. They called him Freddie. The girls had fun that winter, both in school and at home with baby Freddie. Spring came, and with it, a chance to plant again. But the grasshoppers had laid their eggs, and now they were back, eating every live plant in sight. When Pa and Ma saw the grasshoppers again, they became discouraged. Then another opportunity arose. Some friends from

church, the Steadmans, were buying a hotel in Burr Oak, Iowa. They asked Ma and Pa to help them run it. A new settler named Keller bought their house and farm along Plum Creek. The Ingalls family packed up and moved southeast.

On the way, they stopped at Uncle Peter and Aunt Eliza's farm near South Troy, Minnesota. They were not needed in Burr Oak until the fall, so they would stay and work on the farm for the summer. Laura loved playing with her cousins Pete, Alice, Ella, Edith, and Lansford. And she loved her daily chores of watching the cows and guarding the haystacks. As the cows grazed, she and her cousins played along the banks of the Zumbro River, gathering and eating the sweet, juicy plums.

The only dark note was the worry they all felt about little Freddie. He was a weak baby, and often sick. Laura could only hope that he would grow stronger before it was time to pack up and move on to Burr Oak.

THREE

A Terrible Illness

1876–1879
Iowa–Minnesota

It was late summer, and the Ingalls family was deeply sad. Laura's baby brother, Freddie—less than a year old—had been sick for months, and on a dreadful day in August 1876, he died. Losing babies in those times was not uncommon, but it still affected the family powerfully, and they all mourned his death. He was buried at Uncle Peter and Aunt Eliza's farm in Minnesota, under a small white gravestone. When autumn came, they had to leave even that reminder behind; they packed up their wagon and headed to Burr Oak, Iowa. They were on their way to help the Steadmans at their hotel.

To Laura, the hotel seemed very grand. On the street level, there was a parlor, the hotel office, and a tavern. Right off the parlor was a big bedroom occupied by the hotel's wealthiest boarder. Down below were the kitchen, the dining room, and a sleeping area. Upstairs, there were four small bedrooms.

Life at Burr Oak was busy from morning until night. Guests were always coming and going; they lined up in the dining room to get their meals. The hotel was also used for weddings and dances. Some people lived there permanently; they were called steady boarders, and the hotel establishment took great pains to keep them happy.

Laura's jobs included going out behind the barn to the springhouse to retrieve butter and eggs. The one-room springhouse was built over a brook. The cool water maintained a constant temperature inside the house all year long. Perishable food would not spoil as quickly.

Laura and Mary also made beds, washed dishes, and waited on tables in the dining room.

Ma and Pa were busy all the time too. There was plenty of work for everyone at the inn.

Pa and Ma didn't like the noisy tavern and the constant flow of people. And they especially didn't like the saloon right next door. To Ma, saloons were nothing but trouble: rough men, rough language, and bad behavior. Late one night, the saloon caught fire. Ma quickly woke Mary, Laura, and Carrie and hustled them outside. The girls stood and watched as the bucket brigade—men who stood in a line by the town pump, passing pails of water along to

douse the flames—was finally able to get the blaze under control. Ma and Pa were so grateful that the fire had not spread to the inn and that none of their family had been hurt. But they were still frightened.

After that, Pa and Ma didn't want to live so close to the saloon, so they moved from the inn to a redbrick house that stood near an oak forest. Pa bought a cow, and it was Laura's job to take her out to the pasture in the morning and home again at night.

One day, Laura came home late from an errand that had taken a long time. There she found a brand-new baby sister, with Mary's blond hair and Pa's blue eyes. Ma named her Grace Pearl.

Now that the family had four girls, Pa had to work even harder to make ends meet. Though he could always get work as a carpenter or help out on a farm, he still needed more money. Laura did not fully understand this. Her family lived in a nice house. They had enough to eat, and they were happy. They were not poor. Or were they? Other people in town seemed to think so, and one of them, Mrs. Starr, asked if she could help them out by having Laura come live with her. Her own girls were grown and gone; she was lonely and wanted Laura's companionship. Laura was horrified. Leave Ma and Pa, and her sisters? Never! She was so glad when Ma thanked Mrs. Starr for her kindness but said no, they could not spare Laura.

Clearly, they needed to do something. And Laura had a hunch that she knew what it was: Pa was hankering to set out again. Laura knew just how he felt, because she shared his passion. "No one, who has not pioneered, can understand the fascination of it . . . storms, blizzards, grasshoppers, burning hot winds, and fires . . . yet it seemed that we wanted nothing so much as we wanted to keep going west!" she later wrote. Yes, life on the prairie was hard. But they all had pulled together to make the best of it.

In the fall of 1877, the Ingalls family made the long journey from Iowa back to Walnut Grove, Minnesota. Their arrival in town was celebrated as a kind of homecoming, and they were invited to stay with their good friends the Ensigns until Pa could build them a house of their own. Pa and Ma knew the family from church, and Laura knew their children—Willard, Anna, and Howard—because they had often played together. Doubling up was a common practice on the frontier, and no one seemed to mind making room for neighbors until they could get back on their feet again.

Almost immediately, Pa found a job in a store. And because he was such a skilled carpenter, he was able to get carpentry work on the side too. Ma took care of baby Grace, and she helped Mrs. Ensign with all the chores. Mary, age 13, Laura, age 10, and Carrie, age 8, went off to school every day.

Just like before, Laura was happy in school. She was quickly reacquainted with her old friends and sometimes rivals, like Nellie and Willie Owens. And she made friends with the newcomers too. The children of Walnut Creek were a rowdy bunch. Before class began in the mornings, and during recess, they had raucous snowball fights and fast races. Laura loved all the activity and energy; she jumped right into whatever game her classmates were playing.

Not Mary. She never wanted to join in. Unlike

Laura, Mary was a lady. She even tried to keep Laura from acting so adventurous. One day, Laura was rushing out to join a snowball fight that was already in progress. Mary grabbed Laura by the hair to keep her from going out. But Laura would not be stopped. She just dragged Mary to the open door, and the two girls were both pelted with snowballs. When she finally broke free, Laura ran out into the snow so she could get her revenge on her attackers.

Even though she was a "wildcat" (her cousin's word), she was an excellent student. She loved history and spelling and could often outspell the whole class when the teacher arranged spelling bees. Pa bought her a new schoolbook—she had to share it with Mary—for 61 cents. The book was all about the history of the United States. Laura read it avidly and was very proud when Pa informed her that some of his ancestors had come to Plymouth Colony on the *Mayflower*.

Thing▮▮▮oing well for the family. In the spring o▮▮▮ught a patch of land in the pasture be▮▮▮ new hotel owned by a man named William Masters. Pa then had the taxing job of building a new house. Ma was so glad to have her own place again. She loved the Ensigns, but enough was enough. Although she missed farming, she was grateful that they could stay in one place for the time being. Now Pa could play the fiddle in the evenings again; he taught the girls how to dance, and sometimes they even performed for company.

Later that spring, he got the notion that Walnut Grove needed a butcher shop. During the long, cold winters, people used up their store of cured meats and needed more. So he opened one, though he continued to do his carpentry too.

Laura stayed in school, which ran right through to the summer. Ordinarily this would have made her very happy, but she found herself constantly irritated by a snobby girl from New York, Genevieve Masters, who was the niece of the teacher, Sam Masters. Pa told her to ignore Genevieve, but she just couldn't do it. Genevieve soon became rivals with Nellie Owens. Both girls tried to gain control of all the others at school; it became a fierce competition between them.

Laura kept aloof. Though Genevieve tried to sweet-talk her and Nellie tried to bribe her with little gifts from the store her father owned, their tactics did not work. Somehow, Laura's independent spirit caught the attention of the other girls. To her surprise, she soon found that she was the most popular girl of all. And it wasn't just the girls who courted her favor. The boys always wanted her to play with them: ante I over,

pull away, prisoners' base, handball, and base-
ball. There was only one boy in the school who
could run faster than Laura.

The school term ended in June, and Laura,
now 11, was offered a job. Mrs. Masters asked
her to work at the hotel, where she would earn
50 cents an hour, waiting on tables, washing
dishes, making beds, and looking after Mrs. Masters's grandbaby. Laura liked her work. During
the quiet times between meals, Mrs. Masters let
her slip off to read. Laura made her way through
a big stack of the *New York
Ledger*, a weekly paper,
losing herself in their
exciting stories.
She didn't know
it, but her future
life as a writer
was already begin-
ning, right there
amid the pages

of those newspapers. When she was all done with her chores and her reading, she could walk across the pasture to her home.

Other people in Walnut Grove began to notice what a good worker Laura was: careful, responsible, and capable. Soon she was running errands and doing all sorts of odd jobs for friends and neighbors. The nickels and dimes she earned made her—and her parents—proud.

On Sundays, the Ingalls family attended the Congregational church and Sunday school, and in the afternoons, Laura went to services at the Methodist church as well. The Methodists were offering a prize to the girl or boy who could repeat the golden text and central truths from the Bible. This was just the sort of challenge Laura loved. There were 104 verses to remember, and Laura was determined to master them all. Like in a spelling bee, the children tried to recite all the verses, only to fail and be disqualified. Finally, just Laura and one other boy were left—

both had recited the verses perfectly. Although there was just one prize Bible, the minister's wife told Laura that if she was willing to wait, a nicer, even fancier version would be ordered and given to her. Laura agreed—it was a prize worth waiting for.

Laura had just turned 12 in the winter of 1879 when Mary suddenly became very sick. She complained of a throbbing in her head, and her fever spiked so high that Ma cut off all her lovely blond hair—the hair Laura, a brunette, had always envied—in a desperate effort to cool her down. The doctor came, but he could do nothing to help her get better. Ma and Pa were sure she would die.

Laura was afraid for her sister. They were so close. Sometimes they quarreled. Sometimes Laura was jealous, because Mary was so pretty and well behaved, while she thought of herself as plain and stout. But despite that, Mary was her best friend, and she loved her sister deeply.

They had already lost Freddie. What would happen if Mary died? Laura couldn't bear to think of it.

The exact nature of Mary's illness was never determined but it was severe enough to have damaged her optic nerve and it caused her to go blind. But Mary surprised them. She was strong and pulled through. Although she was only 14 years old, she did not complain or mourn; she seemed to accept her sightlessness and was deeply grateful for the love and support of her family.

When it was clear that Mary would never be able to see again, Pa took Laura aside. He had something very important to ask. Now that Mary was blind, Laura must act as her eyes. Through Laura, Mary would keep in contact with the world, and it would be Laura's job to describe the things that her sister could no lon-ger see. Laura was quick and lively, so Pa had confidence in her. Laura nodded very solemnly in response to Pa's request. She knew it was a big responsibility, but she was ready to take it on. She would do as Pa asked, now and always.

Laura's new role was helping her to grow up. And although she did not know it, making pictures with words for her sister was preparing her for what would be her life's work: it was turning a bright, observant girl who loved reading into a full-fledged writer.

FOUR

A Train Trip and Life on the Prairie

1879–1882
Dakota Territory

Not long after Mary had gone blind, a surprise visitor drove up to the house. Laura did not recognize her, but she turned out to be Aunt Ladocia, Pa's sister. Aunt Docia had come from Wisconsin. Her husband worked for the railroad, and they were heading west. She offered Pa a job managing one of the company stores owned by the railroad. Pa said yes immediately, but Ma made him promise that once they moved to the Dakota Territory, they would finally stay put.

Pa sold the farm and left with Docia. Laura and her sisters stayed behind with Ma. With Pa gone, Laura helped in every way she could. She did chores, packed their belongings, and took Mary for long walks. Soon it was time to leave. They would take a railroad trip to Tracy, Minnesota—a first for the girls. The train ride was so exciting. Laura loved every little thing about it. She faithfully described it all to Mary so that Mary could "see" it along with her.

Pa met them at the train station in Tracy, which was in the Dakota Territory. He'd been working all summer long, selling goods to the railroad workers from the company store and keeping track of their hours too. But now the railroad men had finished their work and would be moving on. Pa would go with them. Once again, the whole family joined a wagon train heading west. They traveled about 40 miles until they reached the new railroad camp. It was built on the edge of a lake, and when Ma saw the moonlight glimmering on the water, she called it Silver Lake. That was not its real name, but it stuck in Laura's mind, and she used it to title her book *By the Shores of Silver Lake* many years later.

Ma, Pa, and the girls

settled into a log shanty, which was a crude wooden shack set apart from the bunkhouses where the workers lived. Ma didn't trust the railroad workers, men who broke up the prairie sod and leveled the uneven places to get the land ready for laying the tracks. She told Laura and her sisters to stay away from them.

Laura wanted to be good and obey, but she was fascinated by the monumental work of building the railroad. One day, Pa took her out to see how it was done. She was so curious, she could have watched all day. But when she went home to tell Mary about it, Mary did not seem very interested.

Mostly, Laura tried to mind Ma and stay away from the workers. It was not all that hard because there was so much to do at home. As summer turned to fall, the railroad work on nearby Silver Lake was just about done. The men were packing up and getting ready to go east for the winter. In the spring, the new tracks would

be laid down. Ma and Pa thought they, too, might head east. But then Pa got an offer from one of the surveyors. He wanted Pa to stay on to guard the equipment and supplies. Pa would get a salary, and the family could live in the surveyor's house for the winter.

The house, larger than any house they had lived in before, had two stories, several rooms, and glass windows. The doors had china knobs. Best of all, it was bursting with food: barrels of flour, cornmeal, and salt pork, as well as

salted fish, dried apples, potatoes, beans, and boxes of
soda crackers. There were
even treats like pickles
and jarred peaches. No one
would go hungry in *this*
house.

They settled in for the
winter. Ma and the girls
did their sewing and
knitting while Pa went
out hunting and look-

ing for a homestead. At night he
played the fiddle, or someone read
aloud so Mary could enjoy the stories
too. One night Pa came home and said
he'd found the homestead he wanted. It was
just a mile from the town of De Smet, so the
girls would be able to go to school. As soon
as he could get to the office, he would file a
claim. This meant that Pa would apply to the

government to keep the land he'd chosen. The government would give him the land for free if he agreed to build a home, farm the land, and remain there for at least five years.

Christmas came, and with it, a visit from a couple named Robert and Ellie Boast. Pa knew Robert Boast from the railroad work. Boast had planned on going to Iowa for the winter, but when he heard Pa was going to be in De Smet, he changed his mind and decided to stay as well. He and his bride moved in to one of the abandoned shacks in the railroad camp to wait out the winter. It was good to have neighbors during the long, cold months of snow and sleet. Mrs. Boast was young, pretty, and lots of fun. Laura was looking forward to spending time with her.

Early in 1880, lots of would-be homesteaders began arriving on the prairie. Since the surveyor's house was the only building for miles around, Ma found herself offering hospitality to strangers day and night. She and Pa let the weary and hungry travelers sleep on the floor and share their meals. Soon they began charging for the privilege—25 cents for a meal, 25 cents to lay their bedding by the fire for the night.

The house turned into a crowded, noisy place with strangers coming and going all the time. Laura helped with the cooking and washed mountains of dishes. Mrs. Boast helped out too.

It was hard work, but the Ingalls family was happy with the money they earned.

Money was an even bigger issue than usual right now. Ma had heard of a college for the blind, and she wanted to send Mary there. But unless they could come up with the tuition, and money for room and board, it would not be possible. Ma had even hinted that she hoped Laura—who continued to be an excellent student—would become a schoolteacher when she turned sixteen. A teacher's salary would add considerably to the amount of money set aside for Mary's education. Laura did not want to be a teacher. The thought of it filled her with despair. But she was willing to do it if it meant Mary could have this opportunity.

Once again, Ma's love for learning led the way. Back in the nineteenth century, schooling was not common or even considered necessary for women. It was enough for them to learn the domestic arts needed to run their households and raise their children. Sewing, knitting, cooking, baking, and cleaning were thought to be more important than reading, writing, history, or math. So for Ma to insist on an educa-  tion for *all* her girls, even a blind one, for whom expectations were far lower, showed that she was something out of the ordinary.

Among the many people who passed through the house that late winter and early spring was Reverend Alden from Walnut Grove. He had come to start new Congregational churches all along the railroad line. Ma recorded the first church service, which was conducted in the surveyor's house, as having taken place on February 29, 1880.

In March, Laura and Carrie walked into the town of De Smet. They did not see much—only a lot of sticks poking out of the ground. Ma explained that those sticks were marking the places where all the houses and shops would be built. Pa bought some land along the main street. There he built two wooden stores. One he sold, and the other he kept. But soon he realized town was a place to spend only the winter. He and the family were itching to get out onto the prairie, to settle on the land for which Pa had filed a claim in February.

He began building a shanty on it as soon as he could find the time. First he dug a shallow cellar, and above it he erected a wooden frame. Then he hung the frame quickly, with rough boards, and added a slanting roof. The shanty was very small, and it wasn't even finished when they moved in that spring. But Laura was glad to get back to the prairie.

The flowers opened in a riot of pink, blue, and yellow, and the fresh breeze felt good on Laura's face. The first night they slept there,

Pa dreamed that a barber was cutting his hair. Sleepily, he put his fingers up to the spot and woke up at once when he realized he held a mouse in his hand! He threw it against the floor so hard that he killed it. In the morning, he found the shorn patch where the mouse had been busy. He wanted to get a cat, but cats were scarce on the prairie. In *Little Town on the Prairie*, Laura uses this anecdote—only, in her fictionalized account, the family got a kitten and their problems with mice were over.

There was plenty of work for Pa to do. He

covered the rough frame of the shanty with black tar paper and filled in the holes in the walls to keep out the cold and rain. Then he dug a well and built a stable for the cow. When that was completed, he drove to Lake Henry and came back with a whole box of seedlings. Laura helped plant them. When they grew, they would provide shade and protection from the wind. Next there was the job of planting the garden. Pa used his plow to break up the thick prairie sod.

Laura was so busy helping plant the new garden that she didn't get back to town all summer. To her surprise, winter came early on the prairie: on October 15, a fierce blizzard tore through the area. The howling winds and snow lasted for three days. Pa was worried. Here it was only October and they had been hit with such terrible weather. The shanty was flimsy, with thin walls. How would they manage for the rest of the season?

Pa and Ma decided they would move into town for the winter. They loaded up the wagon and took everything to the building Pa had built on the corner of Main and Second streets. It was sturdy enough to withstand the elements, and they were able to settle in before November 1, when De Smet's first school started its session. There were fifteen students in all.

The blizzards continued to sweep across the prairie. Since little towns like De Smet depended on trains for deliveries of food, coal, and other supplies, a storm that dumped snow

on the tracks caused delays that interrupted the flow of daily life. School had to be closed, and the railroad said it was shutting down service until spring. The food supply in De Smet dwindled. Pa told Ma and Laura that the last sack of flour in town sold for $50.00 and sugar was going for $1.00 a pound, which was much more than their usual cost. Since there was no coal, people burned wood instead. But Pa had a better plan: he and Laura twisted hay into ropes and burned that. It was not easy work. Laura's hands grew chapped, red, and covered with sharp cuts.

The winter of 1881 was known as the "hard winter" because there were so many blizzards—more than usual. Laura was 14, old enough to help Ma and Pa now. Staying warm and fed was a daily struggle. Laura tried to keep her own spirits up, as well as those of her sisters.

The snow did not let up until April, and the train did not resume service until May. Finally, the Ingalls family was able to return to the homestead they had left months before. Pa built two more rooms onto the shanty. And he planted wheat and corn in the hope of harvesting a good crop.

It was at some time during this year that Mary, Carrie, and Laura had their first photograph taken. Few people back then owned cameras; cameras were big, clumsy, and expensive. Instead, they dressed up in their best clothes and went to a profes-sional photographer who would take a formal portrait.

Soon there was more talk of sending Mary to school. Reverend Alden knew all about the Iowa College for the Blind. He had a relative who taught there. The school offered high school – and college-level courses to blind students. It taught them the skills they needed to be independent and take care of themselves. During the summer of 1881, Ma and Pa began to make preparations for Mary's departure.

Laura was eager to help. Instead of spending the summer on her beloved prairie, she took a job in town, sewing at the dry goods store. She had never had to sit still for so long, and she hated it. Her shoulders and neck ached, she pricked her fingers with the needles, and her eyesight grew blurry. Still, she did the best she could

60¢

10 ¢

36¢

and took pride in earning money for her family. By the end of the summer, she had made a whole $9.00 to contribute to Mary's school wardrobe. Ma wanted her to keep some of the money, so she bought a plume for her bonnet (60 cents), a thimble (10 cents), and four yards of calico cloth (36 cents).

In the fall, Ma and Pa got into the wagon with Mary. They were going to take Mary to school in Vinton, Iowa. Saying good-bye was hard. But Laura knew Mary had to go. She took her sisters and went back into the house. Although leaving Mary was hard for Ma and Pa, seeing the school comforted them. They liked everything about it: the big, redbrick building, the walkways where students could stroll, and the farm that bordered the campus. They were equally impressed by the courses: natural history, science, math, economics, music, and politics. And they appreciated the practical side of the curriculum that taught sewing, weaving, and beadwork. Mary would learn to make hammocks, and fly nets for horses. She would be able to support herself in the future.

It was lonely for Laura back in De Smet without Mary. She was so used to her company. She tried to take comfort in her younger sisters, and in her schoolwork, which was very important to her. She was 15 years old now. At 16, she would get her teaching certificate, and the pay she would earn would go a long way toward helping Mary.

Laura made friends with several of the girls at school: Mary Power, Minnie Johnson, and Ida Brown. But there was one girl she did not like—Genevieve Masters. Laura remembered her from Walnut Grove. Genevieve had been mean back then, and she was just as bad—or even worse—now.

Genevieve was not the only problem Laura had at school. The teacher, Miss Eliza Jane Wilder, was not able to keep the classroom under control. Then Genevieve began spreading nasty stories about Laura, and Miss Wilder believed them. Laura was worried. These stories might prevent her from getting her certificate.

But lucky for Laura, Miss Wilder did not

stay long. She was replaced by Mr. Clewett, Mr. Seeley, and Professor Ven Owen. Under the guidance of these teachers, Laura excelled. She did especially well in history and writing. Even during the summer back at the homestead on the prairie, she kept up her schoolwork. She was determined to get that certificate so Mary could stay at college in Iowa. And when Laura was determined to do something, nothing could deter her from her goal.

FIVE

Married Life

1882–1892
Dakota Territory–Florida–Missouri

In December of 1882, Laura's school put on an exhibition. The whole town was invited to hear the students recite pieces from memory, give readings, and perform other demonstrations of their classroom skills. Because she was one of the oldest and best students, Laura was given a big part. She had to recite half the story of America's history. Her friend Ida Brown had to recite the other half. Laura was very nervous. But to her great relief and delight, she did extremely well. She knew all her facts and did not forget anything. Everyone clapped loudly and praised her performance. The evening was a triumph.

A few weeks later, the Ingalls family had two visitors: their friend Mr. Boast and his cousin Mr. Bouchie. To Laura's astonishment, Mr. Bouchie was there to offer Laura a two-month job teaching at a small school in a settlement about 12 miles south of De Smet. Mr. Bouchie did not care that she wouldn't be 16 until February. He needed teachers right away and he wanted to hire Laura, so he told her not to mention her age to anyone. Her salary would be $20.00 a month. That seemed like so much money!

Twelve miles and back was too far to travel on a daily basis. If Laura accepted the position, she would have to live with Mr. and Mrs. Bouchie, which she did not want to do. But Laura thought of her sister Mary, and of how hard her parents worked to keep her in school. She said yes.

There were only five students in her new

class, and Laura did her best to teach them. She modeled her lessons on her own classroom in De Smet, and she did her own schoolwork while the students were working on their lessons. The worst part was living with Mr. and Mrs. Bouchie. She felt unwelcome in their house and was homesick for Ma, Pa, and her sisters.

When the weekend came, Laura despaired. There was no escaping the gloomy and unfriendly Mrs. Bouchie. But, happily, she found

a surprise visitor at the schoolhouse: Almanzo Wilder had come with his buggy and offered to drive her home. Laura knew Almanzo from town. Sometimes he had walked her home from church, and he had a pair of beautiful horses she had always admired. His sister had been her teacher in De Smet.

For the next eight weeks, Almanzo came faithfully to pick Laura up on Fridays and then drove her back on Sundays. When the two-month job ended, she was grateful to go back to her own lessons at school. She did very well, and her teacher, Professor Ven Owen, was extremely proud of her. He told Ma and Pa that she was exceptionally bright and that she should further her education.

Laura continued seeing Almanzo Wilder. He was 10 years older than she was, and he was a homesteader with 320 acres of land. His family had farmed in Minnesota and New York State. When he told her that his brother called him

Mannie and his parents called him Manzo, Laura did not like either of those names. She decided to call him Manly, and so a new nickname was born.

Laura and Manly had a lot of fun together. He bought another pair of very fast, frisky horses he called Skip and Barnum, and they pulled the buggy quickly along through town, over the prairie, and to places like Spirit Lake, where there were ancient Native American burial grounds. In the winter, they took sleigh rides around town; Laura loved being outdoors in the brisk, bright weather.

In the summer of 1884, Manly proposed to Laura and gave her a gold engagement ring set with pearls and garnets. Ma said that she was not surprised; she had known it was coming. She and Pa gave Laura and Manly their blessing.

Laura and Manly didn't marry right away. Laura was still in school, and Manly had to take a long trip with his brother Royal to visit

their parents in Minnesota, and to the New Orleans Exposition in Louisiana. He would not be back for months. When he left, Laura missed him very much. He missed her too, and he showed up on Christmas Eve, saying he could not be apart from her for so long.

In the spring of 1885, Laura agreed to teach one more term of school. Since married women were not allowed to teach, she would have to give up her career after the wedding. Her new job was at the Wilkins School, where she earned $30.00 a month for a three-month term and got to live with the Wilkins family, whom she liked.

She was glad to give this money to her parents to help with Mary's expenses.

Even though Laura had accepted Manly's ring, she still had doubts about being a farmer's wife. From Ma's experience, she knew all too well just how hard a life it was: lots of work, and very little money. Manly listened to her concerns and asked that they give farming a try for three years. If they had not succeeded by then, he'd give it up.

His words must have calmed Laura's fears. On August 25, 1885, Laura and Manly drove to Reverend Brown's house and were married.

Laura was too independent of spirit and mind to accept the word *obey* in the wedding ceremony, and so she did not utter it. Manly agreed with her.

After the wedding, they drove to Ma and Pa's for dinner. Laura might have had mixed feelings about starting a new chapter in her life; she loved Manly but would miss her parents and sisters very much. When the time came, she bravely kissed them all good-bye. She was a married woman now, and she went home to the house that Manly had built for them, just two miles north of De Smet.

Laura loved the little gray frame house. There were windows in the kitchen, the living room, and the bedroom. In the pantry was a special cabinet Manly had designed and made. Now that Laura would be running her own house, she could put all Ma's lessons to good use.

Despite her earlier doubts, Laura was excited about the farm she and Manly were planning. To save money, Laura started helping with the work. She learned to use different machines and rode the corn binder, driving six horses. When they weren't working, they visited friends or Ma and Pa in De Smet. They went to concerts and church socials. Sometimes they saddled up their two swift ponies, Trixie and Fly, and rode off across the prairie. Other times, they took

buggy rides. Laura loved the red and pink wild roses blooming all around her.

In the summer of 1886, Manly looked over his wheat field with satisfaction and pride. He had never seen such a promising crop. But in August, before he could harvest the wheat, a terrible storm blew across the prairie, and hail came pounding from the sky. The wheat field was destroyed. There would be no big harvest that year. He and Laura were bitterly disappointed.

But there was good news too. Laura was expecting a baby, so she and Manly had to change their plans. On their first anniversary, they mortgaged the little gray house and moved into a shanty on another part of their claim in order to save money. Manly continued to farm, making plans for the next year. Laura could not help anymore. She had to rest while she waited for the baby.

On December 5, 1886, Laura gave birth. Thinking of the lush flowers she had seen over the summer on her rides with Manly, she called the baby Rose. Rose was a big, strong baby, and Laura

was grateful for that. But the spring and summer of 1887 were again disappointing. The crops were poor, and a fire destroyed the barn and a lot of the hay. Laura thought they should give up farming. Pa had, and he and Ma now lived full-time in town, where he worked as a carpenter.

Manly was still not ready to give up. He told Laura they needed to keep working and be patient. The next year, though, things got even worse. Laura and Manly came down with diphtheria. Diphtheria is a bacterial infection spread by coughing or sneezing. It affects the nose and throat, and the disease makes breathing difficult. Today there is a vaccine that prevents the spread of diphtheria. Back in Laura's time, the vaccine did not exist and the disease could be serious, even fatal.

They were nursed by Manly's brother Royal. Little Rose was taken to town, where her loving grandparents watched her. Even though both Laura and Manly survived, their recovery was slow, and Manly was never the same afterward. His hands and feet were partially crippled, and walking was difficult for him. He could no longer manage the 320 acres, so he sold part of it, and he and Laura returned to the gray house. Peter Ingalls, Laura's cousin, moved to De Smet. He was a big help to Manly, and they were able to plant some crops.

The summer of 1889 was hot and dry. The wheat and oats withered, shriveled, and finally died. Laura and Manly had one good thing to look forward to: another baby was on the way. Sadly he was born one stifling day and died 12 days later; Laura never even gave him a name.

For the remainder of the summer, Laura mourned her loss. She wanted only to rest. She began to rely on Rose, who was almost four, for simple chores, like feeding the stove with hay sticks. One day, the hay Rose carried caught fire. Terrified, she dropped it, and the fire immediately spread. Laura couldn't even rally to put out the fire. All she could do was escape with Rose. By the time Manly rushed in from the field and the neighbors came to help, it was too late. The little gray house had burned to the ground.

Manly built a shanty near the scorched, blackened place where the house had been. But it was only a temporary dwelling. There was another drought, and Manly still was not fully recovered. He and Laura decided they would go to Minnesota, to his father's thriving farm. Help was always needed there. The Wilders packed up what little they had left after the fire and traveled by covered wagon to Minnesota.

Manly's family welcomed them with open arms, and Laura quickly grew to love her in-laws. Laura and Manly stayed for about a year but were advised that a warmer climate might be good for Manly's crippled hands and feet. Laura's cousin Peter had moved to Florida. He wrote, urging them to come. They decided to give it a try. Once again, Laura and Manly were on their way. This time they went by train, well stocked with food given to them by the generous Wilders.

To Laura, Florida might as well have been the moon. With a mixture of fascination and revulsion, she described a place "where butterflies are enormous, where plants . . . eat insects . . . and alligators inhabit the slowly moving waters." While she tried to adjust, Manly may have worked in the lumber camps near Westville, or he may simply have tried to recover his strength. But Laura could not get used to Florida.

The moist, dense air made her feel sick. Their new neighbors shunned the Northerners, whom they called Yankees. She took to carrying a revolver in her skirt pocket and did not let Rose out of her sight. Laura longed to go home.

So in 1892, after less than a year, the Wilders packed up again and took the train back to De Smet. They stayed with Ma and Pa before moving to a house just a block away. Manly did carpentry or painting, or he worked as a clerk in Royal's variety store. Laura worked at a dressmaker's shop, where she earned $1.00 a day. Little Rose stayed with her grandparents. Ma taught her to sew and knit. At the age of five, Rose started attending the De Smet school, and like her mother, Laura, she was immediately recognized as an unusually gifted student. Laura was proud of her.

At night, after work, Laura and Manly tried to come up with another plan. Large-scale farming was out of the question now. If they were going to farm, it would have to be on a much smaller scale. And they needed a place that was not too cold. They started to hear about land in the Ozark Mountains of Missouri. One of their neighbors had visited the Ozarks. When he came back, he brought a shiny red apple. Laura had never seen an apple so big or so red. Surely that must be a sign of something good. She and Manly agreed. Missouri was the place to be.

SIX

A Budding Writer, and Rose Leaves Home

1894–1903
Rocky Ridge, Missouri

On a morning in July of 1894, Laura, Manly, and Rose were ready for their trip to the Ozarks. There had been a big farewell dinner at Ma and Pa's the night before. The family had all gathered together; even Mary was home from school. After they ate, Pa sang and played the fiddle.

Laura was nervous about the long ride in the black painted wagon. But she was somewhat comforted by the knowledge that she had a $100 bill stashed safely away among her things. This was money she had earned working for the dressmaker, and she was counting on using it to buy a piece of the inexpensive land available in Mansfield, Missouri. One other comforting thing she had with her was a small diary, purchased for 5 cents. She thought it would be interesting to keep a record of her travels.

The Wilders were joined on the trip by the Cooleys, a family they had met in De Smet. Starting from De Smet, the two families went south to Yankton, South Dakota, which was on the Missouri River. They had to cross the slow, muddy river on a ferry. They continued south, and then east, through Nebraska and Kansas. The prairie

was hot and dry, as it always was in the summer. In her diary, Laura wrote that the temperature often reached 100 degrees or more.

On August 22, they left Kansas and crossed the Missouri state line. Here was a big change. Missouri was rolling and green. The hot, dry wind became a cool, gentle breeze. There were trees, not just dry plains. Laura wrote letters back to her family in De Smet, describing everything. In her signature bright, lilting style, she also wrote to Carrie Sherwood, editor of the *De Smet News and Leader*. The letter ran in the paper, and Ma clipped it and sent it to Laura, who was so proud of her very first publication.

After weeks on the road, the Wilders and the Cooleys reached Mansfield. The Cooleys went off to a hotel. They were going to be innkeepers. The Wilders camped out, looking for a farm. Almost immediately, Laura fell in love with an abandoned little farm about a mile outside of town. Manly thought it looked neglected. Laura saw the potential in the land and the apple orchard. Using the $100 bill as a down payment on the $400 farm, she persuaded Manly to see things her way. They paid the bank, and the place was theirs. Because of all the rocks on the property, Laura called it Rocky Ridge Farm.

They moved in

right away. There was a log cabin already built. It had no windows, so light came in from the chimney, or through chinks in the mud that held the walls together. Laura and Rose worked to make the cabin comfortable and pretty, while Manly chopped down trees, both to clear the land and to build up a store of wood for the winter.

The Wilders planned to grow fruit and raise chickens and cattle. They saw farming as a joint effort, one in which a man and a woman worked side by side, together. The same woman who did not want to promise to obey was one who saw herself as an equal. Manly's hands and feet had improved, and he could do more work now. Together, he and Laura cleared the brush and timber from their land. They used some of the fallen trees to make fence rails and to build a henhouse and a barn. Manly sold some of the wood for 75 cents a load. That money, along with the money Laura earned from selling eggs, kept them going that first year.

In the spring, they planted corn and a garden. Rose helped by gathering eggs and the wild huckleberries and blackberries. At age 8, Rose was old enough to take buckets of berries into town to sell for 10 cents a gallon.

Because Rocky Ridge Farm was so close to town, Rose was able to go to school. Just as Caroline had communicated her love of books and learning to her daughters, Laura did the same for her own daughter. Everyone thought Rose was the smartest student in

the class. She was an excellent reader and speller, too. She brought home books like *The Five Little Peppers and How They Grew*, *The House of the Seven Gables*, *The Life and Adventures of Martin Chuzzlewit*, and *Pride and Prejudice* from the school library. At night, Laura read them aloud.

On Sundays, there was no school or work, and the family relaxed. If the weather was nice, they had picnics with the Cooleys in the ravine near their cabin. Laura and Manly taught Rose to ride a horse, and they bought her a donkey named Spookendyke. Rose was supposed to ride him to school and back, but he was sluggish and stubborn. How she hated those rides!

Life at Rocky Ridge was good. Laura and Manly were able to buy another six acres of land as well as a cow and a pig. Laura and Rose churned butter that they sold for 10 cents a pound. And they had extra vegetables to sell to town folk. The orchard was doing well, thanks to all the research Laura and Manly did about apple growing. They added peach and pear trees and planted strawberries and raspberries in between the rows.

They were able to expand the log cabin too. First Manly added a frame room with actual windows and a door. Later he and Laura selected a new building site a short distance from the log cabin. Manly then removed the new room from the old cabin and, using big logs, rolled it onto the new site. When that was done, he built another new room right next to it and joined the two rooms together. Up above he created a sleeping loft for Rose. The old log cabin was turned into a barn.

Life at Rocky Ridge was not all work. There were corn-husking parties, barn dances, and quilting bees. Laura loved to dance. "There is always a little music in my feet," she said. These gatherings included an abundance of food. Laura's contribution was usually gingerbread.

She used an old recipe of Ma's; the result was soft, moist, and delicious. At home, Laura made gingerbread for special occasions like birthday or holiday dinners.

One year, Rose asked if she could make the gingerbread for Manly's birthday. Laura said yes, she was old enough now. Rose was excited and vowed to be extra careful in the baking. Sometimes when Laura left her to watch the bread, Rose got caught up in a book and the bread burned. Not today. She made the gingerbread, and when she took it from the oven, she thought it looked every bit as good as Laura's. Laura and Manly were away for the day, but how proud Laura would be when Rose served the gingerbread.

Then Rose was surprised by an unexpected call from the minister. She served him a piece of the gingerbread and noticed he had an odd expression on his face as he ate. He said no to a second piece. Rose wondered about this until she and her parents ate their own pieces later that evening. Rose had mistakenly used cayenne pepper instead of ginger! The gingerbread burned their mouths, but they had a good laugh about it.

During the late 1890s, Mansfield was growing fast. There were general stores, hotels, a bakery, a drugstore, an opera house, flour mills,

and a bank. Although Rocky Ridge was prospering, it was not yet a fully self-supporting farm. Laura and Manly decided to leave it for a while, and they rented a little yellow house just outside of town. Manly went to work as a drayman, or deliveryman, hauling loads and picking up goods transported by railroad. Laura took in boarders and started making country-style meals using ingredients from the farm, like fresh eggs, milk, fruit, vegetables, and chickens raised on Rocky Ridge. She served them to the travelers staying at the yellow house and invested her earnings back in the farm. As soon as they had enough money, they would return.

Rose became a town girl. She was not sorry to say good-bye to her stubborn old donkey. But she was sad to think she would have to end her studies after eighth grade. The school in Mansfield did not go any higher, and while there were private academies in other towns, Laura and Manly could not afford the tuition.

In the summer of 1898, Grandpa and Grandma Wilder came for a long visit. They were heading south, to settle in Crowley, Louisiana. Manly's sister Eliza Jane had married the wealthy owner of a rice plantation. Before he left, Grandpa bought the yellow house and turned the deed over to Manly.

Laura's family was doing well too. Ma and Pa wrote to say that they were snug and comfortable in their house in De Smet. Mary lived with them now. She knew Braille, a system of raised dots that enabled blind people to read, and she was a big help to Ma with the housework. Carrie worked at the *De Smet News and Leader* office. She, too, lived at home with her parents. Grace was a country schoolteacher, and in 1901 she married a man named Nat Dow.

In the spring of 1902, things took a sharp turn for the worse. Ma wrote to say Pa was suffering from heart failure. Laura left Rose in charge of the household and quickly got ready to travel back to De Smet. She arrived in time to see Pa, who lingered briefly and then died in June. Ma and all the girls were with him until the end.

Laura mourned her beloved Pa. She had  so many fine memories of him. In all her books, Pa is shown as kind, loving, cheerful, and fun. He told stories. He played the fiddle. He could hunt, trap, and build or fix just about anything. Now he was gone.

Still grieving, Laura stayed in De Smet for a while before going back home. She missed her father but took comfort in her husband and daughter. Yet Rose was soon ready to leave Mansfield. Her aunt Eliza Jane had invited her to Crowley, Louisiana. If she lived in Crowley, she could go to high school and even study Latin. Laura could see how much the opportunity meant to Rose, so she and Manly agreed to allow Rose to live in Crowley for a year. A brilliant student, Rose crammed four years of Latin into one, and she graduated from high school in 1904. At the ceremony, she recited an original Latin poem she had written. Clearly, Rose was a very bright girl, with many opportunities open to her.

But once she was back in Mansfield, Rose's opportunities seemed to shrink. Although she was a high school graduate, she could not get a job. Rose wanted to help her parents, who were still struggling to make ends meet. Without a job, that was not possible. And she wanted to go to college. How would she manage that?

Then she saw her chance. The depot master in town agreed to teach her and his own daughter telegraphy. The electric telegraph was a communication system that transmitted electric signals over wires from location to location that translated into a message. Long before the Internet, fax machines, or the telephone, telegraphed messages were the way people communicated over long distances.

Rose picked up the skill easily. She got a job as a telegraph operator in Kansas City, Missouri, for $2.50 a week. That was enough money to support herself and to help her parents, too, so at the age of 17, Rose left home.

SEVEN

Building the Dream House

1904–1924
Rocky Ridge Farm, Missouri

After Rose moved to Kansas City, Laura and Manly remained in the little yellow house. But when Manly's parents died and left him $500, they decided to sell it and make some improvements to the house at Rocky Ridge Farm. Laura had so many ideas. She was particularly eager to use the materials found on the land, like the rocks and timber. So she sketched out her plans for a ten-room farmhouse with four porches, a beamed parlor, a library, and a stair-case that led to the second level.

The new house took two years to complete. Laura loved the fireplace, which was made of three slabs of native rock. Manly had not been keen on the fireplace. Laura had to fight for it; she even broke down crying. She was determined to get her way—and in the end, she did.

She also got a new kitchen, with all its cup-boards and drawers to keep clutter out of sight, an oak-paneled parlor, big glass windows, a library, and a small office off the kitchen where she could write letters and keep the farm's account books. It was her dream house.

The farm was thriving. Apples, pears, strawber-ries, and raspberries grew abundantly. The Jersey cows were sleek and healthy. They gave milk that the Wilders sold at market. Laura's flock of Leghorn hens laid eggs throughout the winter, when no one else's hens did. Laura

began to get invitations to speak about her methods at farmers' clubs.

On one occasion, Laura was too busy to give her speech, so she wrote it and sent it off to be delivered in her absence. John Case, the editor of the *Missouri Ruralist*, was in the audience. He liked Laura's style so much that he asked her to start submitting articles to his magazine.

Laura was surprised. She had always loved writing but never thought of herself as a professional. Since she had nothing to lose, she decided to try. "Favors the Small Farm Home," her very first article, appeared in the February 1911 issue of the *Ruralist*.

After that, she began to write regularly for the *Ruralist*. Essays, poems, feature stories, and interviews with country people all flowed from her pen. And she still found time to cook,

clean, and do all her farm chores. Laura earned between $5.00 and $10.00 for each piece that she wrote. Soon she had a column of her own, called "The Farm Home." Later, she had another called "As a Farm Woman Thinks." Readers often wrote in to praise her articles and essays. The editor told her that he preferred her stories to everything else in the magazine. Laura was so proud. Soon she began writing for other publications too.

Rose, now all grown up, was also a writer. She had done a lot of traveling while she was

Rose

working for Western Union Telegraph. In 1909, she married Gillette Lane, and they moved to Kansas City. Now she had a job as a writer for the *Kansas City Post*.

Kansas City was not too far from Mansfield, so the couple came to Rocky Ridge for a visit. Rose took comfort in seeing her parents. Like Laura, she'd had a baby boy who died. She was very saddened by his death. Being with her mother made Rose feel better. While she was there, Rose offered Laura guidance about her writing. She told her to get someone else to take care of the chickens so she could devote more time to it. They discussed other aspects of writing too, such as techniques and story ideas. Laura was so proud of Rose. And she trusted her advice.

When Rose and Gillette left Rocky Ridge, they did not go back to Kansas City. Instead, they went to San Francisco, where Rose had a new job writing for the women's page of the *San Francisco Bulletin*. Laura could not believe her daughter's good fortune. Rose interviewed celebrities of the day, like Henry Ford, who started an automobile empire that still exists today, and Charlie Chaplin, a silent film star. In 1915, Rose wrote to Laura asking her to come out west for a visit. Manly was not able to make the trip, so Laura went alone.

At first Laura was worried about leaving Manly. He assured her he would be fine. Laura

boarded the train for California. She stayed for two months, and while she was there, she wrote letters to Manly about the marvelous new things she was experiencing. Like she had done for Mary all those years before, Laura was using her words to paint pictures for someone else. But she had an even clearer goal now. In one of the letters, she told Manly that she planned on doing "some writing that will count." She was 48 years old, and her life was about to take an important new turn.

When Laura got home, she continued writing her columns. She urged farmers' wives to become active partners in their farms. Her inspiration was her own mother, who had shared the burdens and the joys with her father as an equal. And Laura's own marriage to Manly was structured in much the same way. This came at a time when women all over the country were organizing and marching for their rights, including the right to vote, which they did not get until 1920.

Laura observed that farm women had always been partners with their husbands; no one had given them proper credit before.

Soon Laura began to expand her intellectual activities beyond her writing. She worked to create circulating libraries and social events for farm women. In 1916, she helped found a group called the Athenians and, as a member, was involved with the creation of a country library. The group also put on literary programs about William Shakespeare, Charles Dickens, and Mark Twain.

Meanwhile, Rose was becoming even more famous as a writer. She divorced Gillette but used his last name when she published her books and articles. She never forgot her mother's faith in her. She dedicated her book *Peaks of Shala* "To my mother, Laura Ingalls Wilder." Rose had clearly inherited her love of words from both her mother and her grandmother. Just as Laura was influenced by her own mother, Rose was influenced by Laura. She was another link in the chain of strong, smart women in her family.

Rose continued her busy life. She traveled to Paris, to other parts of Europe, and to Asia. In 1923, after four years away, she returned home to Rocky Ridge in time for Christmas. She set up her typewriter in an upstairs room and got to work. Her plan was to earn enough money to allow her parents to retire. She also encouraged Laura to write for better-paying magazines like *McCall's* and *Country Gentleman*. Laura took her advice and was happy with the checks she received. Her career as a writer seemed to be going well. But she had no way of knowing that the best was yet to come.

In 1924, Ma died, and Laura felt her loss keenly. She noted the profound influence her early life had had on her: "The example set by my mother and father has been something

I have tried to follow, with failures here and there, with rebellion at times, but always coming back to it as the compass needle to the star." It would take a little longer, but soon those early experiences would come together in a great and glorious vision.

The Little House Books

1928–1957
Missouri–California–South Dakota–Missouri

By 1928, Rose was convinced that her parents were too old for farming. Laura was 61, and her father 10 years older. With Rose's urging, they hired a man to help with the work. He brought his family to Rocky Ridge and became a good friend.

Rose, who was very successful by this time, paid for the building of a new house for her parents. The brown and tan rock cottage had five rooms and was wired for electricity—no more kerosene lamps. The furniture was not hand-made but ordered from a department store. And the Wilders even got a car—another gift from Rose.

Reflecting on all these things, Laura could scarcely believe the changes she had seen in the course of her own lifetime. She thought of her childhood as a pioneer girl on the prairie. It was a way of life that had completely vanished. Laura felt strongly that her experiences needed to be shared and that they were too important to be lost. So in 1930, she decided to write her autobiography.

She began with her family's move from

Wisconsin to Indian Territory and ended with her marriage to Manly. Laura called her story *Pioneer Girl* and gave it to her daughter to edit. Rose made suggestions and typed up her mother's handwritten pages before giving them to her literary agent in New York City. The agent did not think a publisher would buy it. Then Rose tried sending it to a magazine, to run in installments. Again she had no luck. This was discouraging news. Laura had to wonder whether her stories would ever be published.

Finally, a friend of Rose's suggested that Laura's story might be more suited to children. So Laura rewrote it, calling it *Little House in the Big Woods*. And to her great surprise and greater delight, Harper & Brothers agreed to publish the book. It first appeared in 1932. She did not have great expectations "but hoped a few children might enjoy the stories I had loved."

More than a few children did. The book was an immediate success. Children loved it. So did teachers, librarians, and booksellers. *Little House in the Big Woods* was so popular that Harper asked for a second book. Laura responded by writing *Farmer Boy*, which was about Manly's childhood. It appeared in 1933. Once again, it was a great success, and Laura began work on *Little House on the Prairie*. (Many people think this was the first book in the series, but actually it was the third; it came out in 1935.) She wrote in between making meals and doing housework. She did not use a newfangled typewriter, but a pencil and lined school tablets that she bought at the grocery store for 5 cents each. And she was a serious scholar, intent on getting all the details right.

Now Laura had an even bigger idea. She wanted to do something that had not been done before:

a series of books for children. It was her aim to record everything she could about her early life on the American frontier. Her publisher, Harper, thought this was a good plan. The next book in the series was *On the Banks of Plum Creek*, which came out in 1937. That same year, Laura and Manly moved back to their big old farmhouse. (Rose left Rocky Ridge for the University of Missouri, in Columbia, where she was doing historical re-search). They had missed it all this time. Laura set up her study off the bedroom and began planning the next books in the series.

Many people don't know that Laura's first illustrator was Helen Moore Sewell. Sewell had studied at Pratt Institute in Brooklyn, New York, and was very popular at the time. She illustrated the first three books; for the next ones, she collaborated with Mildred Boyle.

Laura was becoming famous. Her editor, Louise Raymond, wanted to meet her. And she wanted Laura's readers to meet her too. Laura traveled to a book fair in Detroit, Michigan. A big crowd came to hear her speak. Afterward, she signed copies of her books and answered questions.

When she got back home, Laura began the next book, *By the Shores of Silver Lake*, which was published in 1939. She and Manly also took a long trip with some friends out to the Pacific Coast and back through South Dakota (the Dakota Territory of her childhood had been made into a state in 1889). Laura wanted to revisit some of the places she was writing about.

After this trip, Laura and Manly stopped traveling. They felt they were too old. Though

Laura's hair was white, her mind was still sharp. And she kept busy with chores, like cooking, baking, and churning. Laura received fan mail with letters and drawings from the children who loved her books. She enjoyed their letters, and because she did not want them to feel disappointed, she answered them all. And she kept writing: *The Long Winter* (1940) was the next book. It was followed by *Little Town on the Prairie* (1941) and *These Happy Golden Years* (1943).

Five of Laura's books were named Newbery Honor books (*On the Banks of Plum Creek, By the Shores of Silver Lake, The Long Winter, Little Town on the Prairie*, and *These Happy Golden Years*)

Laura earned a lot of money from the sales

of her books. She and Manly were well off and no longer worried about how they would get by. But Laura was now 76 years old, and when her publisher asked for still another book, she said no. After 11 years of steady writing, she felt she was done.

People have very different points of view about Rose's role in the creation of the Little House books. Some people say that they came entirely from Laura and that Rose provided only encouragement and access to agents and editors. Others say that Rose took the rough drafts and quietly transformed them. Still others think that both points of view contain some truth.

For 20 years before the publication of the first Little House book, Laura had already proved herself as a professional writer. Rose was a gifted editor, and her skills were well known and in demand. Like Laura and her own mother, Rose and Laura were very close; it would have been natural for them to discuss their writing and turn to each other for advice and guidance. The Little House books were most likely the product of an unusual collaboration. Laura had the raw material (which Rose also used for her novels for grown-ups, such as *Young Pioneers*, *Cindy*, and *Hillbilly*) and was a good storyteller. Rose had a flair for dramatic pacing and overall structure. If Laura had not written the books, they would not exist, because Rose had no interest in writing for children. But if Rose had not edited them, it is quite possible they never would have been published.

When Laura stopped writing, she and Manly settled into a quiet, contented routine. They still worked in the house and garden. They spent

time with friends, played board games, and read. Laura had a keen interest in politics and world events, and she continued to follow both. Mary had died in 1928, four years after Ma. Grace died in 1941. Laura and Carrie, the two remaining sisters, made sure that Pa's fiddle was preserved in a museum in South Dakota. When Carrie died in 1946, Laura was the only Ingalls sister left.

Occasionally, Laura thought about writing another book. But she didn't actually do it. (*The*

First Four Years was written around 1940 but not published until 1971.) She was pleased, though, when the existing books were reissued in 1953. This time, they would have new illustrations by Garth Williams, the artist who had illustrated *Charlotte's Web* and *Stuart Little*. When Williams was commissioned to do the illustrations, he was not familiar with any of the places in the books. So he took a trip with his camera and his sketch pad to see them. He recorded landscapes, birds, trees, animals, houses, and towns. He also

went to Missouri to meet Laura. Originally, the editor wanted Williams to create eight oil paintings for each of the books—64 in all. But it turned out that would be too expensive. Instead, he used pencil, charcoal, and ink to create the illustrations that have by now become an indelible part of the Little House world. The warm, almost fuzzy look they have seems to perfectly capture the cozy, homespun quality of the Ingalls' lives.

In July 1949, Manly had a heart attack. He was 92 and frail. He survived and even seemed to be getting better. But in October he had another attack, and this time he died. Laura missed him terribly. "It is quiet and lonely here now," she wrote to a friend. But she remained at Rocky Ridge, where she continued to receive acclaim and honors.

In 1951, people in Mansfield, Missouri, decided to name the local library after her.

Although she was not strong, Laura wanted to be at the ceremony. She showed up with her white hair piled high on her head, secured by a gold comb that matched her gold earrings. Her dress was red velvet and very fine. She wore an orchid pinned to one shoulder and looked younger than her 84 years.

Although Laura continued to miss Manly, she found comfort and joy in the love of her ever-widening circle of readers. At the age of 87, she took her first airplane ride, to Danbury, Connecticut, where Rose was living. In 1957, Laura celebrated her 90th birthday. She received cards, letters, greetings, and gifts from all over. It was a wonderful tribute.

But Laura was not well. Three days after her birthday, she died. All over the world, people mourned the loss of the pioneer girl who had grown into one of America's best-loved writers.

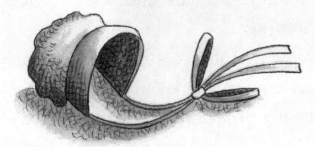

Epilogue

Although Laura died almost 60 years ago, her name is more famous and beloved than ever. Her writing has kept her alive. Altogether she wrote eight books in the Little House series. Collections of letters and diaries exist as well. Her books have remained in print, have been translated into more than 40 languages, and continue to delight new generations of children all over the world.

A successful television series based on the books began in 1974 and ran through 1982. It starred Michael Landon as Pa, and Melissa Gilbert as Laura. The show inspired a spin-off series called *Little House: A New Beginning*, in which new characters appeared. There were also three made-for-television movies: *Little House: Look Back to Yesterday* (1983), *Little House: Bless All the Dear Children* (1984), and *Little House: The Last Farewell* (1984).

Today, people still read her books, watch the movies and the television shows, and visit the places that she immortalized through her words. Museums, historic sites, and homesteads are all preserved and maintained in Burr Oak, Iowa; De Smet, South Dakota; Independence, Kansas; Mansfield, Missouri; Pepin, Wisconsin; and Walnut Grove, Minnesota, places that had meaning in Laura's life. Even though the events she wrote about happened a long time ago, today's readers still find her stories of the American frontier, with its hardships and joys, as exciting as ever.

Quotes from Laura Ingalls Wilder

Laura was a plainspoken, forthright woman who had a lot to say about life and how to live it. In her letters, diaries, and interviews, she shared her thoughts and feelings about the world. These quotes, taken from multiple sources, make clear her down-home philosophy, one in which simple pleasures and the love of family and friends are the most important things of all.

*It is the sweet, simple things of life which are
the real ones after all.*

*Every job is good if you do your best
and work hard.*

Home is the nicest word there is.

*If enough people think of a thing and work hard
enough at it, I guess it's pretty nearly bound to
happen, wind and weather permitting.*

*Once you begin being naughty, it is easier to
go on and on, and sooner or later something
dreadful happens.*

*It is still best to be honest and truthful; to make
the most of what we have; to be happy with
simple pleasures and to be cheerful and have
courage when things go wrong.*

Remember me with smiles and laughter, for that is how I will remember you all. If you can only remember me with tears, then don't remember me at all.

Suffering passes, while love is eternal. That's a gift that you have received from God.
Don't waste it.

The trouble with organizing a thing is that pretty soon folks get to paying more attention to the organization than to what they're organized for.

It is not the things you have that make you happy. It is love and kindness and helping each other and just plain being good.

There's no great loss without some small gain.

The only stupid thing about words is the spelling of them.

It is a good idea sometimes to think of the importance and dignity of our every-day duties. It keeps them from being so tiresome.

Remember well, and bear in mind, a constant friend is hard to find.

Games Laura Played

Laura, her sisters, and her friends played all sorts of games outside. Some of them, like softball and tag, will be familiar to you. Others will not. Here are the rules for some of their favorite games; try them yourself!

Ante I Over

To play this game, you'll need a ball that has enough weight to be thrown far but is not heavy enough to break a window. Divide the players into two teams. The teams take their places on either side of a small building with a two-sided

slanted roof. One team throws the ball over the roof and calls out, "Ante I over." When the ball comes across the roof, the other team tries to catch it. If the ball is caught, the team has to run around to the other side of the building and throw the ball at a player to claim him or her as their own player. If the team does not catch the ball, a player throws the ball back over the roof while calling out, "Ante I over." The goal of the game is to capture all the players from the opposing team.

Pull Away

Imagine two 20-foot-long lines that are about 50 feet apart from each other. All the players line up on one line or the other. One person is "It." That person stands between the two lines and calls out to both sides, "Pump, pump, pull away, come out or I'll pull you out." Players from both sides try to race to the other side without getting caught by "It."

While the players are racing to the opposite side, "It" tries to catch one of the players by tapping her lightly three times on the back. If this player cannot get away before "It" has finished tapping, this person also becomes "It." Now when the lead "It" calls out the same phrase, the players again try to get safely to the other imaginary line. Both "It" people can catch these players and tap them three times gently on the back. Anyone caught becomes "It." Sometimes a number of "It" people will gang up on a person to catch her.

The goal of the game is to be the last person caught. The last person caught becomes "It" for the next round of the game.

Prisoners' Base

Imagine two 20-foot-long lines that are about 50 feet apart. These lines are considered "home." About a yard's distance in front of each of these lines is another imaginary line about one yard long. This is the prisoners' base.

The players are divided into two teams. They line up on these imaginary home lines facing each other. The game starts by players leaving their home lines and going out between the two home lines, taunting each other to be tagged. The last person out from the home line is the "freshest" player, so he or she is able to tag a "less fresh" player from the other team.

Team players will try to cover each other by "freshening" themselves before going after an opponent player. When a player is tagged, he becomes a prisoner on the other team's prisoner base. The prisoner needs to stand on the prisoner base but may stretch out from it as far as she can in order to touch a rescuer.

Now her team will try to rescue her before her team player is tagged by an opposing team player. If a rescue player manages to touch the prisoner before the rescuer is tagged, the prisoner and the rescuer are free to go home without any interference. The goal of the game is to make all the players of the opposing team prisoners of your own team.

A Prairie Craft: Corn-Husk Doll

Wherever corn was grown as a crop, children in both pioneer and Native-American families used the husks to make dolls. Since Laura's family often grew corn, it's quite possible that she and her sisters made and played with dolls like these. Follow the simple instructions below to make a corn-husk doll of your very own.

YOU WILL NEED:

- string
- scissors
- a bucket of water

* bags of corn husks (these can be purchased already cleaned, dried, and in uniform sizes at a craft store)

1. Soak corn husks in a bucket of water until they are soft and easy to work with.

2. Arrange four corn husks as they appear in this drawing.

3. Tie the tops together with a short piece of string.

4. Cut the ends so that they are rounded.

5. Flip over and pull the husks down over the cut ends.

6. Use string to form the doll's head.

7. Flatten another husk and roll it tightly.

8. Secure each end with string to form arms for the doll.

9. Slide the arms inside the husk as shown.

10. Form a waist by cinching the middle with string.

11. To make shoulders, fold a husk over the arms and torso in an X shape.

12. Arrange four or five husks around the waist, with the straight ends on top, to create a skirt.

13. Secure the skirt with string.

14. If you would like to make legs, use small strips of husk as shown in the illustration. Tie small strips of husk around any exposed string (neck, waist). Use fabric scraps to make clothing, and yarn for hair.

What Laura Ate

People back in Laura's time ate some dishes that would be familiar to us and some that would not. Here are a few recipes for foods Laura mentions in her writings that she and her family might have eaten.

Gingerbread

Laura and her family loved gingerbread. Gingerbread was their celebration cake, made for birthdays and holidays. Gingerbread is moist, spicy, and delicious.

YOU WILL NEED:

  2 cups all-purpose flour, sifted before
    measuring
  ⅓ cup sugar
  1 teaspoon salt
  ½ teaspoon baking powder
  1 teaspoon baking soda
  1 teaspoon cinnamon

1 ½ teaspoons ground ginger

½ teaspoon ground cloves

½ cup melted butter

1 cup molasses

1 egg

½ cup buttermilk or sour milk (To make sour milk, combine ½ teaspoon vinegar and ½ cup milk, and let mixture stand for 5 minutes)

¼ cup hot water

1. Preheat oven to 350°.

2. Sift together the flour, sugar, salt, baking powder, baking soda, and spices.

3. Stir in the melted butter, molasses, egg, and buttermilk or sour milk.

4. Beat in hot water.

5. Pour batter into a generously greased and floured 8-inch square pan.

6. Bake for 45 to 50 minutes, until cake springs back when lightly touched.

7. Serve warm with whipped cream.

Johnnycakes

There are many references to johnnycakes in Laura's books; they were a staple of the family's diet. A johnnycake is a type of cornbread that can fit easily into a saddlebag without crumbling or getting crushed, so it was ideal to take along on the many journeys across the plains.

The original recipe probably came from the Native Americans, who often shared their food with the settlers. They may have originally been called *journey cakes*, a name that would easily have been corrupted into *johnnycakes*. Or the name may be a corruption of *Shawnee cakes*, named for the Shawnee tribe of the South and Midwest. Still others say it is a corruption of an ancient Indian word, *jonikin*, and that it came to us by way of the Narragansett tribe of Rhode Island. But whatever the origin of their name, johnnycakes are delicious and easy to make. Below is an old-fashioned recipe like the one that Laura and her family might have used.

YOU WILL NEED:

    1 cup stone-ground cornmeal (white or yellow)
    1 teaspoon salt
    ½ teaspoon sugar (optional)
    1 cup boiling water
    Butter (or bacon drippings, oil, or other fat)
    ½–1 cup milk

1. Whisk together cornmeal, salt, and sugar (if used).

2. Bring water to a boil and pour over the meal

mixture, whisking to prevent lumps.
Let batter rest for 10 minutes.

3. Butter a large skillet or griddle and bring it to a sizzle, taking care not to let the butter burn.

4. Add enough milk (½ cup to 1 cup) to the batter to make it the consistency of mashed potatoes, and drop by spoonfuls several inches apart (they will spread) to make cakes about 2 or 3 inches wide.

5. Let the cakes gently sizzle on the skillet for 6 to 11 minutes, until they are a deep golden brown on the bottom and slightly firm on the top.

6. Add more butter to the skillet, and/or place a thin pat of butter on each cake, before turning them over and cooking for another 6 minutes (or longer if necessary), until they are a deep golden brown color. Serve with butter and maple syrup.

Makes about 8 cakes.

Homemade Butter

Back when Laura was a girl, butter was made in a round wooden churn with a long pole to work the cream. Today, it would be hard to find an old-style butter churn. But you can still make delicious butter by following the directions below. Use it on your johnnycakes.

YOU WILL NEED:

1 pint heavy whipping cream
1 clean glass Mason jar with lid
2 medium-size bowls
1 spatula

1. Leave the cream out on the counter for 20 to 30 minutes, then pour it into the Mason jar.

2. Put the lid on the jar and start shaking it. After about 2 minutes, you'll see a nice, lightly whipped cream.

3. After about 4 minutes, the contents of the jar will look like thick whipped cream.

4. After about 9 minutes of shaking, the cream will start to separate from the sides of the glass. You might want to take a short break.

5. After about 14 minutes, the whey will have begun separating from the butter.

6. After about 16 minutes, the curd will be more noticeable, and there will be much more whey.

7. Start pouring off the buttermilk into one of the bowls. You can drink it or use it in another recipe. Continue shaking the butter for a few minutes, until your butter has solidified a bit more and until you aren't getting any more buttermilk.

8. Pour out the butter into a bowl. It will look like a scoop of ice cream.

9. Pour cold water over the butter and start "massaging" it with a spatula to rinse the rest of the buttermilk out. Continue replacing the water until the water stays clear. Drain.

10. Spread your fresh butter on crackers, bread, or johnnycakes!

Little House Books
by Laura Ingalls Wilder

Little House in the Big Woods (1932)

Farmer Boy (1933)

Little House on the Prairie (1935)

On the Banks of Plum Creek (1937)

By the Shores of Silver Lake (1939)

The Long Winter (1940)

Little Town on the Prairie (1941)

These Happy Golden Years (1943)

The First Four Years (written around 1940, but published in 1971)

Other Writings by Laura Ingalls Wilder

On the Way Home (1962) This is a diary of a trip to Missouri Laura and her family made in 1894. It was published after her death.

West from Home (1974) This is a collection of letters from Laura to her husband, Manly, written in 1915 and published after Laura's death.

A Little House Traveler (2006) This consists of three parts: *On the Way Home* and *West from Home*, as mentioned above, and *The Road Back*, a previously unpublished diary.

Glossary

Calico—A brightly printed cotton cloth imported from India.

Diphtheria—A highly contagious and potentially fatal disease caused by bacteria. Symptoms are a sore throat and fever.

Homestead—A farmhouse with nearby buildings and land.

Husk—The outer shell or covering of some fruits or seeds, like walnuts or corn.

Kerosene—A thin oil made from petroleum, used for heating and cooking and in lamps.

Mortgage—The deed that spells out the financial

agreement between the bank and the owner of a house or building.

Prairie—A large area of flat or rolling, treeless grassland.

Shanty—A roughly built wooden cabin or shack.

Sod—A section of grass-covered soil held together by matted roots.

Surveyor—A person whose job it is to carefully look over, or survey, land.

Whey—The thin, milky liquid that is left after cheese or butter has been made.

Sources

The author used the books below in her research; look for them in your library if you would enjoy reading more about Laura Ingalls Wilder.

Anderson, William. *Laura Ingalls Wilder: A Biography.* New York: HarperCollins, 1992.

Collins, Carolyn Strom, and Christina Wyss Eriksson. *The World of Little House.* New York: HarperCollins, 1996.

Wadsworth, Ginger. *Laura Ingalls Wilder: Storyteller of the Prairie.* Minneapolis: Lerner Publications Company, 1997.

Wilder, Laura Ingalls. *West from Home: Letters of Laura Ingalls Wilder to Almanzo Wilder, San Francisco, 1915.* Edited by Roger Lea MacBride. New York: Harper & Row, 1974.

Zochert, Donald. *Laura: The Life of Laura Ingalls Wilder.* New York: Avon, 1976.